WEAR A HELMET!

HEALTHY SAFETY HABITS

Mary
Elizabeth
Salzmann

Consulting Editor,
Diane Craig,
M.A./ Reading Specialist

Sandcastle

An Imprint of Abdo Publishing
www.abdopublishing.com

www.abdopublishing.com

Published by Abdo Publishing, a division of ABDO, PO Box 398166, Minneapolis, Minnesota 55439. Copyright © 2015 by Abdo Consulting Group, Inc. International copyrights reserved in all countries. No part of this book may be reproduced in any form without written permission from the publisher. SandCastle™ is a trademark and logo of Abdo Publishing.

Printed in the United States of America, North Mankato, Minnesota
102014
012015

 THIS BOOK CONTAINS RECYCLED MATERIALS

Editor: Alex Kuskowski
Content Developer: Nancy Tuminelly
Cover and Interior Design: Colleen Dolphin, Mighty Media, Inc.
Photo Credits: iStockphoto (Slobo Mitic), Shutterstock

Library of Congress Cataloging-in-Publication Data

Salzmann, Mary Elizabeth, 1968- author.

  Wear a helmet! : healthy safety habits / Mary Elizabeth Salzmann.

      pages cm. -- (Healthy habits)

  Audience: Ages 4-9.

  ISBN 978-1-62403-533-3 (alk. paper)

  1. Accidents--Prevention--Juvenile literature. 2. Safety education--Juvenile literature. 3. Health--Juvenile literature. [1. Safety.] I. Title. II. Series: Salzmann, Mary Elizabeth, 1968- Healthy habits.

  HV675.5.S215 2015

  613.6083--dc23

                        2014023600

SandCastle™ Level: Transitional

SandCastle™ books are created by a team of professional educators, reading specialists, and content developers around five essential components—phonemic awareness, phonics, vocabulary, text comprehension, and fluency—to assist young readers as they develop reading skills and strategies and increase their general knowledge. All books are written, reviewed, and leveled for guided reading, early reading intervention, and Accelerated Reader® programs for use in shared, guided, and independent reading and writing activities to support a balanced approach to literacy instruction. The SandCastle™ series has four levels that correspond to early literacy development. The levels are provided to help teachers and parents select appropriate books for young readers.

EMERGING · BEGINNING · **TRANSITIONAL** · FLUENT

CONTENTS

WHAT IS A HEALTHY HABIT?

Staying safe is a healthy **habit**.

There are many
ways to stay safe.

Kylie, Cam, and Addy always wear their bike helmets.

Edwin floats down a river. He wears a life vest.

Lydia is getting a ride to school. She has her seat belt on.

Caleb crosses the street at a **crosswalk**. He pushes the button. He waits for the walk signal.

PUSH
BUTTON
FOR

Ava helps bake cookies. She uses an oven mitt to hold the hot pan.

Zach washes his hands often. It helps keep him safe from **germs**.

Sam never shares private **information** with strangers online.

What do you
do to stay safe?

HEALTH QUIZ

1. Staying safe is not a healthy **habit**. True or False?

2. There are many ways to stay safe. True or False?

3. Lydia does not have her seat belt on. True or False?

4. Caleb doesn't cross the street at a **crosswalk**. True or False?

5. Ava uses an oven mitt to hold the hot pan. True or False?

Answers: 1. False 2. True 3. False 4. False 5. True

GLOSSARY

crosswalk – a specially marked path for people to walk safely across a street.

germ – a tiny, living organism that can make people sick.

habit – a behavior done so often that it becomes automatic.

information – the facts known about a person or subject.